I0453134

Kneading Hope:
Lessons from the Kitchen of Life
By Nilla Spark

First published in Australia in 2025 by
Nilla Spark
Albany, Western Australia 6330

FMG Press - Nilla Spark
ISBN: 979-8-9928190-6-9
Kneading Hope:
Lessons from the Kitchen of Life

Graphic design and supplementary photography by Wayne Harrington.

Printed by Advertiser Print.

A Journey Through Food, Family and Hope

LIFE is not just a collection of moments, but a recipe crafted from the ingredients of our challenges, triumphs, and the people who shape us along the way. This book is an invitation to step into my world, where food, family and healing intertwine to create something far greater than the sum of its parts.

For all of us, life has a way of breaking us in ways we never expect. Loss, pain, and heartbreak carve deep into our hearts, leaving wounds that sometimes feel too vast to heal. I understand this all too well. My journey has been one of profound grief – a shattered heart, pieced together time and time again. But within those cracks, I have discovered resilience. In the ashes of pain, I've found the strength to rise again.

The kitchen has always been my sanctuary – my safe space. When words failed me, when the weight of loss threatened to swallow me whole, I found solace in the rhythmic kneading of dough, the gentle stirring of sauces, and the quiet transformation of simple ingredients into nourishing meals. Cooking became my language for hope, a quiet rebellion against despair. It showed me that even in our darkest moments, something beautiful can emerge.

This book is not just a collection of recipes; it is a chronicle of survival, a testament to the power of resilience. With each dish, I share a piece of my story – of losing my mother far too soon, of yearning for children that never came, of battling cancer, and of mourning fractured relationships that left me searching for connection. These pages hold the weight of those losses, but they also hold the hope, love, and healing that have guided me through.

In the kitchen of life, every ingredient has its purpose, even the bitter ones. They shape us, challenge us, and, ultimately, transform us. The lessons I've learned from grief and loss are woven into these recipes, like the careful threads of a tapestry. Each one is a reminder that while we cannot avoid life's heartbreaks, we can choose how we rebuild ourselves in their aftermath.

Cooking is, for me, more than just sustenance – it is a metaphor for life. A pinch of salt here, a splash of olive oil there. In the midst of chaos, it reminds us to slow down, to pay attention to the little things that bring flavours and joy. As I stand at the stove, I am reminded that life, too, is a delicate balance – a dance between sweet and savoury, bitter and bold.

This book is an invitation to step into my kitchen, to stir, knead, and taste alongside me. It is a call to embrace the messy beauty of life, to find hope even when it feels elusive, and to nourish your spirit one dish at a time. My story is one of heartbreak and healing, but above all, it is a story of resilience – a reminder that even from the deepest losses, we can rise, we can rebuild, and we can thrive.

Each chapter is a dish, a lesson, a memory that has shaped who I am and how I see the world. Through these stories, we will knead together the dough of our experiences, adding layers of love, loss, and resilience. We'll rise, just as we do in the kitchen, to create something new – something beautiful – a life richer than we ever dreamed possible.

Join me on this journey, where every dish is a step toward healing, and every page brings us closer to the hope we all seek.

Nilla x

4

CHAPTER 1

A Mother's Final Lesson: Resilience Born of Love and Loss

Shaped by love, forged in loss and carried through every challenge.

THE kitchen was quieter than usual when I returned home after my mother passed. It felt like the world had shifted in ways I wasn't prepared for. Just days before, I had stood beside her, watching her weathered hands roll cavatelli on the tabletop. It was a simple task – flour and water shaped into small, curled pieces – but that moment marked the final lesson she would teach me. As I watched the dough take shape under her gentle touch, I felt an unspoken connection to her – a connection that, even in her absence, would never be broken.

In the week or so before she passed, her words as she handed me her wedding band (that had slipped off her cancer-ravaged fingers) echoed in my mind: "Do and be something with your life, bella mia. Not like me. Here I am at 44 and not achieved anything." She had spoken with raw honesty; with a vulnerability I had never before heard from her. At that moment, I realised that Mama's life wasn't incomplete – it was a beautiful mosaic made of small, quiet sacrifices that created a foundation for the rest of us to rise from.

Mama had always been the heart of our family, her hands tirelessly moving between pots and pans, never pausing long enough to claim credit. At 44, she had lived a life not defined by her own dreams but by duty, love and sacrifice. Her smile often masked the weight of the life she'd led, the unspoken weariness beneath. In those final moments together, those last hours spent in the kitchen, her hands guided mine, showing me how to roll the dough just so, pressing each piece until it curled into itself. "Just like that – see? It holds the sauce perfectly. Cavatelli. Not too big, not too small," she had said.

But there was more. There was something in her eyes that I couldn't quite grasp at the time, a knowing that sat heavily in the room between us. She sat at the end of the table, frail but resolute, her body slowly surrendering to illness,

Mama and I when I was five years old.

6

yet her mind was still sharp. I remember the way she watched me, almost as if she were trying to pass on everything, she could in the time she had left. She knew that there was so much more she had yet to teach me – lessons that could not be spoken aloud, only understood in the stillness, in the rhythm of the kitchen where she had always taught me how to be strong, how to love, how to give.

In those quiet, lingering moments, I felt her words and presence settle over me like the warmth of the pasta we were making. Each curl of dough I rolled felt like an echo of her love, her strength, her sacrifices. It was in those moments I realised that this kitchen, this space where we had always connected, was her final classroom. She had given me everything I needed to continue, but there would always be a part of her that would remain just out of reach.

The cavatelli was no longer just pasta – it was the embodiment of everything she had poured into me, a lesson not only in cooking, but in living, in loving, in carrying on when

Cavatelli in the making.

there was no clear path forward. Each piece of dough, each gentle roll, became my way of holding onto her, a way of continuing the work she had started. The lessons she gave me in life, now held in my hands, would be the ones I would share with those around me, with everyone I meet along this journey. And I would carry them forward, even when I couldn't hear her voice.

Her final lesson to me – "Do and be something with your life, bella mia" – echoed in my mind, a call to action, a call to rise from the ashes of grief. And in the kitchen, in the act of kneading dough and making cavatelli, I began to understand that these small, humble acts of creation were the true essence of what she had always wanted to teach me: that life doesn't stop, even in the face of loss, and that we continue, we rebuild, we love and we keep going.

If something quietly stirred or stayed with you, there's a world beyond these pages where kindred hearts gather. Visit kneadinghope.com.au/stirred when it feels right.

Cavatelli – A Legacy of Family and Heritage

AS my Mama guided my hands in the final moments we shared, teaching me how to knead, shape, and craft the delicate cavatelli, she imparted a lesson that would stay with me forever: the importance of resilience in the face of life's most profound challenges. Her hands, once so steady, now guided mine gently, showing me that life, like dough, is shaped with patience, care and time. In the shape of each cavatelli, I carry her love, her strength and her belief that, even in the darkest times, we can find our way.

CAVATELLI INGREDIENTS:
- 2 cups all-purpose flour
- 1/2 teaspoon salt
- 1/2 cup water (adjust as needed)
- Olive oil (optional for drizzling)

METHOD:
- In a large bowl, combine the flour and salt. Gradually add the water, mixing until the dough comes together.
- Knead the dough on a lightly floured surface for about 5-10 minutes, until smooth and elastic. You want the dough to feel firm but not dry.
- Break off small pieces of dough and roll them into little logs about ½ inch thick. Cut them into small pieces, roughly 1 inch long.
- Take each piece and press it gently with your thumb against a ridged surface (a fork works perfectly), then curl it into a little crescent shape. This is where Mama's steady hands came into play – gently pressing, rolling and shaping.
- Place the cavatelli on a lightly floured baking sheet and let them rest while you prepare the sauce.

MAMA'S SIMPLE TOMATO SAUCE INGREDIENTS:
- 1 can of whole tomatoes
  (or 5 ripe tomatoes, peeled and chopped)
- 2-3 cloves garlic, finely chopped
- 3 tablespoons extra virgin olive oil
- Salt to taste
- Fresh basil leaves, torn into pieces
- A pinch of sugar (optional)

METHOD:
- Heat the olive oil in a large pan over medium heat. Add the garlic and sauté gently until fragrant.
- Add the tomatoes and cook, mashing them with a spoon or potato masher, allowing the sauce to come together.
- Season with salt and a pinch of sugar if the tomatoes are too acidic.
- Simmer the sauce for about 15 minutes, letting it thicken and develop its flavour. Stir in the basil leaves just before serving.

To serve, toss the cooked cavatelli in the sauce, coating them evenly. Serve with a drizzle of olive oil and extra fresh basil if desired.

Cavatelli cooked with a chicken ragu and peas.

CHAPTER 2
Unseen Blessings: From Heartbreak to a New Beginning

In the quiet moments of struggle, we often find the gifts life was waiting to give us.

My precious Mama and me as a baby.

IT all began when I was 32, full of optimism and ready to take the next step in our journey toward parenthood. It was meant to be a simple check-up, just to make sure everything was in place for us to start our family. I had imagined the future would unfold the way it always did in my dreams – carefully planned, with the loving expectation of a child to hold, nurture, and raise. But the doctor's words shattered that dream in an instant.

"You have a one-in-a-thousand chance of conceiving naturally. IVF is your only option," he said, his voice soft but firm. Adoption, he added, wasn't even something we needed to entertain because of our ages.

In that moment, time seemed to slow, and the world felt heavy. I could hardly breathe as I processed what I had just heard. It wasn't just the diagnosis; it was the weight of knowing that the path I had always imagined – becoming a mother in the most natural way – was no longer an option. I was devastated.

That marked the beginning of an unexpected journey – a path filled with five rounds of IVF, each one more gruelling than the last. IVF was still a relatively new procedure at the time, and the subject was almost taboo. I remember lying in a sterile hospital bed for days, each one more draining than the last. The first day was spent undergoing the procedure to extract the eggs. The second was filled with the tension of fertilisation, and on the third, the embryos were placed. I had to endure countless injections, endless blood tests and procedures that took pieces of me both physically and emotionally.

The only visitors during those long, painful days in the hospital were John and my little brother, Gian Carlo, their presence a small comfort in an otherwise isolating experience. It was as if I had become a lab experiment, a freak of nature, trapped in a process so intimate, yet so mechanical.

At the time, it felt like I was hiding a deep, silent secret – one I couldn't share because no one seemed to understand. There was no conversation, no support and no acknowledgment of the pain we were enduring. The world hadn't yet come to terms with the reality that motherhood, whether biological or not, is something every person should experience if they desire it. It wasn't about privilege or luck – it was about the natural yearning to nurture, love and connect.

Each IVF cycle was a rollercoaster of emotions. Hope intertwined with fear, and as each attempt ended in failure, the wound grew deeper. The phone calls from the nurse always began with the same heartbreaking words, "I'm sorry to inform you..." and each one felt like another piece of my dream slipping further away. The weight of disappointment bore down on me, but the hope, no matter how faint, never fully disappeared.

But in the midst of this overwhelming loss, there was an unforeseen blessing that would change everything – John's son, my stepson, Jason. I met him when he was just three years old, and from that moment, he became a ray of light in a time when I had lost so much. While the dream of having a child of my own was slipping away with each failed IVF attempt, Jason brought me the gift of family in a way I hadn't anticipated.

I would watch him grow over the weekends, and it was on these weekends that we shared countless memories – fishing trips, weekends in New Zealand, cheering on his dad as he played cricket, all moments that became my new definition of love. Though I didn't give birth to him, Jason gave me something far more valuable – a sense of belonging, a sense of family and a love that transcended biology.

A day at the beach for the Daniele family in 1972.

While IVF could not gift me the child I had longed for, Jason's presence in our lives filled that void in a way I never expected. He was the son I never had, and through him, I learned that family is not defined by blood, but by the strength of the connections we build and the love we nurture.

When Jason was 19, he called me with excitement in his voice. "Nils," he said, "Guess what? I've met an Italian girl. Her family makes passata and Italian sausages just like you do." In that moment, I understood something profound: the connection we shared through food, through the cultural traditions that had shaped my life, was something Jason had longed for too. What I had once thought could only be passed down to my own child was now being carried forward

11

through him. Through his love for her family's culture, I realised that the very traditions I cherished – cooking together, sharing meals and connecting over heritage – had been woven into his own story. I felt a deep sense of gratitude because in that moment, I realised that family doesn't always follow a straight path. It sometimes comes from the most unexpected places, and love finds its way through the connections we nurture.

In time, I was blessed with Lisa, my daughter-in-law, who became an integral part of our family. From the moment she entered our lives, I saw in her a reflection of love, warmth, and connection that we had always longed for. Her heart, her energy and her devotion to family made her someone I could truly embrace as my own.

Jason, me and John.

Through Lisa, I learned that family isn't defined by blood but shaped by shared experiences, love and understanding. One of the most profound connections we shared was through our food. Like me, Lisa cherished the traditions of our culture – cooking with passion, and using meals as a way to bring people together. I saw how, through her, our family's traditions were carried forward with love, just as I had hoped.

The kitchen, for us, has always been more than just a place to cook. It's where memories are made, bonds are deepened, and where love is passed from one generation to the next. We share the spirit of cooking, the joy of preparing meals, and the beauty of creating new memories together. Through these moments, our family's essence was kept alive, passed down through each dish, each shared experience and the love that was woven into every meal we enjoyed.

Through Lisa's love for her own family and the way she embraced ours, I realized that even though life had not unfolded as I had imagined, it had gifted me something more beautiful than I could have ever dreamed – a sense of motherhood, not defined by biology, but by the love and connection we choose to create. In that realisation, I found a joy that reshaped my understanding of family for the rest of my life.

Looking back, I see that the greatest loss – the inability to have a biological child – became the gateway to a much

The now Family Spark: Lisa, John, Harvey, me and Jason.

12

richer, deeper experience of family and love than I ever imagined. In the faces of Jason, now a son in every sense of the word, in Lisa, my daughter-in-law, who brought even more love and connection into our family, and in our grandson Harvey, I discovered that family is not defined by blood. Jason gave me the gift of motherhood in ways I never expected, and Harvey, our precious grandson, has filled a space in my heart I never knew existed. Sometimes, life's most beautiful moments come in the form of what we once thought we couldn't have.

I see how everything unfolded for a reason. When we face the deepest heartache, the pain of unmet expectations, we don't always realise that something else is quietly taking root. Like a garden blooming in the most unexpected place, our family grew in a way I hadn't imagined. And like food, which has the power to heal, nurture, and bring people together, cooking became my way of sharing love.

A recipe, I've learned, can be more than just a dish – it's an expression of all we've experienced, all we've gained and all we've lost. And when I think of family gatherings, the moments of comfort and togetherness, there's one dish that always comes to mind – my Mama's lasagna.

No matter how tired she was, no matter how many things demanded her attention, Sundays were sacred in our house, and it always began with her preparing lasagna. The rich layers, the aromatic sauce, the way the whole house seemed to come alive with the scent of her cooking – it was a reminder that no matter the struggles or exhaustion, love could always be found in a well-prepared meal.

The best birthday gift from our grandson, Harvey.

Lasagna became not just a meal; it was a tradition, a constant. When life felt uncertain, or when grief weighed heavily on my heart, it was lasagna that reminded me of the strength, love, and care my mother poured into our family. It's the dish that, like our journey, is layered with both heartache and hope, but always with the promise of something better.

And so, in honour of Mama, and in the spirit of love and nurturing, I share her special recipe with you – because sometimes, the most profound comfort can be found in the simplest of dishes.

If something quietly stirred or stayed with you, there's a world beyond these pages where kindred hearts gather. Visit kneadinghope.com.au/stirred when it feels right.

Mama's Lasagna – Layered with Love and Tradition

THIS lasagna – with each layer of pasta, sauce and cheese – mirrors the layers of our lives. Each one is a building block that holds us together, even when we feel we might fall apart. Just as my mother would carefully craft each layer, I have come to realise that family, too, is built layer by layer, moment by moment, through both joy and hardship. This dish is a reflection of the warmth and strength found in the simplest of ingredients, and it holds the stories of our lives within it. Every bite carries a memory, a reminder that the bonds of family are nurtured with time, patience, and love. Just as lasagna needs time to bake and meld, so too do relationships – slowly coming together to create something greater than the sum of its parts.

In every bite, I taste the love that has been passed down from one generation to the next, and I carry that love forward, knowing that no matter what life brings, we will always have the warmth of family, the strength of our connections, and the nourishment of each other. And yet, in every layer, there is also the memory of loved ones lost – my Mama, Papa and brother – those who are no longer here but whose presence still lingers in the fabric of our family. Their absence is felt in the quiet spaces at the table, in the unspoken words, and in the memories we hold close. The warmth of the family we have today is tempered by the bittersweet reminder of those we've lost, whether through death, distance, or broken connections. But through this dish, their legacy lives on, wrapped in the same love and care that built our family in the first place.

FRESH PASTA SHEETS INGREDIENTS:
- 100 grams "00" Pasta Flour per person
- 1 egg per person
- Water to combine
- Splash of oil

RAGU INGREDIENTS:
- 2 shallots
- 4 lamb chops
- 1 side of pork ribs
- 1 chicken maryland
- Extra virgin olive oil
- 2 tins of peeled tomatoes
- 2 x 700g bottles of passata
- Parsley to taste

MEATBALLS INGREDIENTS:
- 500g lean beef mince
- 500g chicken mince
- 2 sautéed shallots
- Salt
- White pepper
- Grated nutmeg
- Fine breadcrumbs
- Chopped parsley
- Grated parmesan cheese
- 2-3 eggs to combine

OTHER INGREDIENTS:
- 8 boiled eggs, 400g cooked peas, 500g mozzarella and 300g parmigiana

METHOD:

• Prepare the pasta: Make a mound of flour on the benchtop, make a well in the centre. Break the eggs into the centre, add a dash of oil and lightly incorporate the flour. Only add the water if the dough is dry and only a little at a time until the dough comes together. Knead the dough for at least 10 minutes until smooth. The dough should feel firm to touch. It is ready when you press the dough and it bounces back.

Rest the dough for at least 30 minutes up to one hour to help relax the gluten. When the pasta has been rested, it is time to start making the pasta sheets. Cut a small portion, flatten with either your hand or a rolling pin. Set the pasta machine on the first setting (which is the widest). Fold the dough in half and pass through the machine, continue to re-feed it through until the dough is shiny and smooth. Change the setting on the machine to the middle setting and pass the dough through until it is nice and smooth again. Move to the second last setting to make lasagna sheets. Cook the pasta to al dente in boiling salted water, then place into cold water to stop the cooking and place on tablecloths to dry the sheets out a little.

• Prepare the ragu: Heat olive oil in a large pan over medium heat. Add onion, and sauté until softened and fragrant. Add the meat and cook until browned. Stir in the tomatoes, parsley, and a pinch of sugar. Season with salt and pepper and let simmer

Lasagna just out of the oven.

for a few hours and you will find that the meat will fall off the bones. It is very important to taste regularly, as you may need to add more salt and if the tomatoes are too acidic, add more sugar. Just keep adjusting until you are happy with the flavour.

• Prepare the meatballs: In a large bowl, mix all ingredients together to create a soft mixture then roll into marble-sized balls. Fry them in olive oil. Once cooked, have them ready in a bowl to be sprinkled in between the lasagna sheets. Boil the peas in salted water and cook until tender. Boil the eggs and ensure that they are hard boiled. Once they are cooled, peel and cut them into small pieces.

• Assemble the lasagna: Preheat the oven to 180°C (350°F). Spread a thin layer of the ragu on the bottom of the baking dish. Place a layer of lasagna sheets, followed by a layer of meatballs, boiled eggs, boiled peas, a generous layer of ragu, then a sprinkle of mozzarella and grated parmesan. Repeat the layers until you have about 6 layers, finishing with a pasta sheet that has been lightly spread with ragu, and sprinkled with mozzarella and parmesan. Cover with foil and bake for 30 minutes then remove the foil and bake for an additional 15-20 minutes until the cheese is golden and bubbly. Allow the lasagna to rest for 10-15 minutes before serving. This helps it set and makes it easier to cut.

CHAPTER 3

The Unfulfilled Heart: My Father's Silent Search

Even in silence, the heart continues to search for what it can never fully find.

My debonair Papa.

LOSS has a way of reshaping a person, and my Papa was no exception. When Mama passed away, she took a piece of him with her. At just 47, he became a widower, suddenly responsible for raising four children and carrying the weight of grief that he didn't know how to express.

Papa was a man of strength, a man who worked tirelessly, almost obsessively, to provide for his family. But in doing so, he didn't have time to connect with us. His love was evident in the things he did – the long hours, the sacrifices, the dedication – but it was never spoken in words. And as a child, I needed more than just the basics. I needed to feel his love in ways that were tangible, in the small moments that told me I was seen, understood and cared for.

Our relationship was always complicated. I often felt like we were two people who couldn't find a way to truly communicate. He was a man of few words, especially when it came to emotions, and that left me feeling distant from him. The wall between us wasn't built from a lack of love – it was built from the grief that he couldn't find a way to process or share. He didn't know how to show the love he felt and I didn't know how to understand the love he tried to give.

Even though we didn't always see eye to eye, I realise now that I inherited so much of him. His stubbornness, his style, his flamboyance – all of these traits were passed down to me. In a strange way, I was shaped by his silent strength. I didn't always understand it then, but now I see how much of his essence I carry with me. His persistence, the way he would keep going even when life was weighing him down, mirrored my own tenacity. And, like him, I tend to forge ahead, even when others can't quite see where I'm going.

After Mama's death, he kept searching for her – in the faces of his children, in the kindness of others and in the quiet moments when he thought no one was watching. But no matter where he looked, she wasn't there. And in that absence, he carried a heavy longing that defined much of the rest of his life.

His health began to fail long before his spirit did. Emphysema took his breath, dimming his dreams and tethering him to an oxygen machine that offered little comfort. Watching him struggle to breathe, a man who had once been so strong, was heartbreaking. But even as his health deteriorated, Papa's love for us remained steadfast. He kept pushing forward, not because he couldn't find the words to say it, but because it was the only way he knew how to protect and provide for his family.

One of the things that stands out most in my memory was how Papa, in his own quiet way, showed his love. Whenever I was coming home to Albany, he would make sure to buy cobbler – the fish I had always loved. He knew it was something I would look forward to, something that would make me feel at home. In his own way, this was how he nurtured me, how he showed he cared when words failed him. I didn't always understand it at the time, but now I see it for what it was: his way of saying "I love you", even if he couldn't speak it aloud.

I remember one particular moment, when Papa, despite his poor health and the doctors' warnings, drove all the way to Perth to see me. I didn't know it then, but he had a plan – he was going to buy us a house. It was his way of showing love, a gesture that only someone like him, with all his pride and self-reliance, could think of. He called me to say he was in town and asked me to come over to the unit where he was staying. I had just returned from a trip to New Zealand, and John, always understanding, insisted I go and see Papa first while he stayed home to sort things out.

When I arrived, Papa greeted me and there, waiting for me, was a plate of freshly made Italian sausage and fried egg. A simple meal, but in that moment, it was everything.

My Mama and Papa, childhood sweethearts.

We sat together, eating in silence, the TV softly playing in the background. Our relationship had never been one for deep conversations, and that evening was no different. Words felt heavy, like they always did between us. But even in the silence, there was a quiet comfort in simply being together. At one point, Papa chuckled softly at something on the television, and I remember how rare it was to see him smile. It was a moment of connection, a glimpse of the man behind the grief.

Then he said he needed some fresh air and stepped outside. That was the last time I saw my Papa alive. Moments later, I heard a crash and ran to find him – a man who had once stood so tall and strong – lying lifeless on the ground.

The next few minutes blurred into chaos. I called for an ambulance, tried mouth-to-mouth resuscitation, and prayed for a miracle that never came. My Papa, the man who had weathered so much pain and loss, was gone in an instant.

But as I knelt there beside him, one thing struck me deeply – the smile on his face. Even in the pain of a heart attack, his expression was one of peace, even joy. It was as if he had finally found what he had been searching for all these years. He had been reunited with Mama, his great love.

In the days that followed, I reflected on the life he had lived, the sacrifices he had made, and the love he had poured into his family in his own quiet, unwavering way. His dream of reuniting with Mama had been shattered in life, but fulfilled in death.

My Mama and Papa holding me as a newborn at the front of our Graham Street home. I think it's fair to say we came from humble beginnings...

If something quietly stirred or stayed with you, there's a world beyond these pages where kindred hearts gather. Visit kneadinghope.com.au/stirred when it feels right.

Italian Sausage and Eggs –
Comfort in Simplicity

Italian Sausage and Eggs.

THIS dish, though simple, is rich with tradition, and it holds a place in my heart that words often fail to describe. It serves as a quiet reminder of the love my Papa had for us, even when the language of that love was not always easy to understand. Like the dish itself, our relationship was often uncomplicated, yet layered with complexities that we never fully had the chance to unravel.

Much like the unspoken moments between Papa and me – those fleeting moments of quiet understanding that didn't need words – this dish brings comfort in its simplicity. As I prepare it, I feel as though I'm bridging the gap between past and present, gently bringing Papa's memory back into my kitchen. Each ingredient, each fold of the dish, feels like a way of honouring him – a way of reconnecting with a love that, though silent at times, was always there, quietly enduring.

For anyone who has struggled to understand a parent, or to be understood, this dish is a reminder that love doesn't always need to be spoken to be felt. Sometimes, it's in the quiet acts, the shared moments, and the traditions passed down that the truest connections are made.

INGREDIENTS:
- 2 large Italian sausages (mild or spicy, as you prefer)
- 2 large eggs
- 1 tbsp olive oil
- Fresh parsley, chopped (for garnish)
- Crusty bread, to serve

METHOD:
- Heat the olive oil in a skillet over medium heat. Add the sausages and cook, turning occasionally, until browned and cooked through (about 10–12 minutes). Remove from the pan and keep warm.
- In the same skillet, crack the eggs gently. Cook until the whites are set, and the yolks are still runny, or to your desired firmness.
- Place the sausages on a plate and nestle the eggs alongside them. Garnish with freshly chopped parsley for a touch of colour and freshness.
- Serve with a slice of toasted crusty bread to mop up the yolk and sausage juices.

OPTIONAL ADDITIONS:
- A sprinkle of chilli flakes for extra heat.
- A side of sautéed spinach or tomatoes for added depth.

19

CHAPTER 4

Timeless Treasures: From Lost Jewels to Recipes That Endure

In the face of loss, some treasures can never be taken - that which we carry in our hearts and the memories we create with love.

MY Mama was a simple, hardworking woman whose family was her whole world. Through me, she lived the life she had only dreamed of - one of travel, adventure, and self-discovery. She dressed me in a way she would have loved to dress herself, always encouraging me to see the world and embrace life's experiences.

In my late teens, Mama often urged me to live fully and not settle down too soon. "Life has so much to offer, Cara mia," she would say. Because of this, I became the black sheep of the family. While my brothers followed the expected path, I was the rebel, exploring beyond the confines of tradition. My Papa struggled to understand my "zingara" spirit – my Nonna's affectionate term for the gypsy soul within me.

Though I was restless, I was far from irresponsible. I worked tirelessly in the restaurant that my parents had built from the ground up. At the age of 16, when Nonna Maria's Restaurant first opened its doors in Albany, everything changed. My parents poured their heart and soul into making this restaurant a reality. My Mama was in the kitchen, working her magic with the food, while my Papa and I were on the floor, nervously waiting for customers to walk through the door. I was still in school, and my life, like my parents', became consumed with the restaurant.

Weekends were a blur of serving tables, clearing dishes, and learning the ins and outs of hospitality. Asking for a night off so I could go out with my friends felt like asking for gold – impossible. Yet, through all of this, I was learning. I was learning responsibility, the importance of hard work, and the value of family. One of my most telling memories of those days was when I was studying for one of my exams, desperate to focus and get some quiet time. I received a call from my Papa, asking me to come to the restaurant immediately because they were overwhelmed with customers. Without missing a beat, I replied, "Papa, I'm studying for my exam," as though that should excuse me from what I knew was important. But to him, nothing mattered more than the family business, and the call was urgent. So without any further hesitation, I put down my books, grabbed my coat and made my way to the restaurant. It wasn't a matter of choice – it was my responsibility.

In those moments, though my dreams of the world beyond the restaurant pulsed within me, I knew the sacrifice was worth it. I was learning a different kind of education – one that could never be taught in school. I helped raise my younger brothers, balancing my academic duties with the daily grind, learning the ways of business and people.

My Mama, my rock, was there in the kitchen, fuelling my courage and determination, always championing me to be unapologetically myself. In her, I saw the quiet strength that would shape me for years to come.

Before she passed, the restaurant flourished after years of struggle. For the first time in 26 years, my Mama returned to Italy, her heart swelling with pride. Papa, deeply moved by their success, adorned her with jewellery – gifts that symbolised their years of sacrifice and triumph. She was radiant, but her joy was fleeting. Shortly after they returned, Mama was diagnosed with breast cancer.

When she passed, I inherited her jewellery – a tangible connection to her love and sacrifices. I would sit and hold each piece, imagining her wearing them, wishing she were still here to enjoy what she had worked so hard to achieve.

Mama and me as a four-year-old at the beach.

Keeping these treasures safe became my priority, so I placed them in the office safe. I trusted that they would be secure there, but fate had other plans. One day, our office was broken into and the safe, bolted to the floor, was ripped out and stolen. Along with it went all of Mama's jewellery and some of my own.

The devastation was unbearable. Those pieces were more than jewellery, they were fragments of my Mama's essence, reminders of her strength and spirit. Losing them felt like losing her all over again.

But grief has taught me that memories are stronger than material things. Though the jewellery is gone, the memories of my Mama remain unshakable – her laughter, her encouragement, her unwavering love. Those are treasures no thief can ever steal.

Many years later, while going through some old papers, I found a handwritten recipe by my Mama for a biscotti called spumette. This simple piece of paper, with her beautiful handwriting, became more precious to me than the stolen jewellery. It was a piece of her, in her own words, a legacy she had left behind.

Now, I can make these spumette in her honour, remembering the hands that once held the pen, the heart that poured love into everything she did. As I bake these biscotti, I carry her memory forward – one recipe, one bite, one moment of love at a time.

If something quietly stirred or stayed with you, there's a world beyond these pages where kindred hearts gather. Visit kneadinghope.com.au/stirred when it feels right.

Mama's Spumette

MAMA'S love was never loud, but found in the quiet, everyday moments –steadfast and enduring. Spumette, a simple almond biscotti, reflects her essence. In every bite, there's a whisper of her spirit, a reminder that beauty doesn't need to be extravagant to be cherished.

These biscotti, with their delicate sweetness, carry the warmth of Mama's hands and the care she poured into every meal. As I bake them now, I'm reminded of her quiet love – the way she made the ordinary extraordinary.

Spumette are more than just a recipe; they're a piece of Mama's soul. Like the stolen jewellery that once held great significance, these biscotti have come to symbolize something far greater. They're not just food; they are a connection to a woman whose love poured into everything she did. And no matter what the world took from us; these simple flavours preserve the love and memories that will never fade.

Each bite of spumette feels like a hug from Mama, a reminder of the sweetness and warmth that remain, and a piece of home I carry forever.

INGREDIENTS:
- 6 medium egg whites
- 450g almond meal
- 450g caster sugar
- 2 teaspoons ground cinnamon

METHOD:
- Preheat your oven to 350°F (175°C). Line a baking sheet with baking paper.
- In a large bowl, mix together the almond meal, sugar, and cinnamon. Gradually add the egg whites to the dry ingredients, mixing until it forms a firm paste - you may not need all the egg whites.
- Roll into balls, size depends on your preference.
- An alternative is to roll mixture into small balls, cover with icing sugar, then pinch the top, or put in piping bag, make a swirl then place either a glazed cherry or whole almond in the centre.
- Bake for 20 minutes.
- Allow biscuits to cool slightly. Sprinkle with extra icing sugar. Store in an airtight container for up to two weeks.

Spumette

6 bianchi di uova
una libra di
mandorle una libra
di zucchero
2 cucchiaini cannella

Mama's handwritten spumette recipe. Right, it was a joy to produce these for a client as a gift from the heart.

HANDMADE WITH LOVE ♡

23

My Mama (third from left in the back row) on the day of her arrival at Fremantle in September 1954.

A very proud little flowergirl (3) at my Zia Eva's wedding.

Mama and Papa at Zia Eva's wedding day in 1958.

Papa "holding up the rock" at a Daniele family outing to Natural Bridge near Albany in 1968.

Nonna Maria's in full swing in 1973.

Nonna Filomena (my Mama's Nonna) and Nonna Nicoletta (my Mama's mother).

It was always a struggle to get my little brothers to take family photos seriously.

Opening night at Nonna Maria's in 1972 with my fellow waitresses, Sandra and Marilyn.

CHAPTER 5

Breaking Free:
A Journey Through Cancer and Into Life

In the face of uncertainty, food became my language of love and the bridge that connected me to those who helped me heal.

THE moment I walked into the doctor's office, I felt it - an unspoken truth hung in the air like a storm cloud. My heart pounded, hoping for reassurance but the words I feared most tumbled into the silence. "Nilla, I'm sorry..." I interrupted, completing the sentence she didn't need to finish. "I have breast cancer, don't I?" Her nod confirmed it. In that instant, my world tilted on its axis. I fell into John's arms, sobbing, overwhelmed by a tidal wave of fear and disbelief. "I'm going to die," was all I could think!

Memories of my mother's battle with breast cancer surfaced, stark and painful. I was haunted by the idea of John as a widower, of leaving him to manage our life, our home, our business without me. My mind spiralled into chaos. This wasn't part of the plan.

I had convinced myself I was immune. Despite my doctor's warnings – my family history, my IVF treatments, the fact that I hadn't breastfed – I had waved them all away. "It won't happen to me," I had thought. But it had. Through the tears and fear, one thing became clear – I wasn't ready to give up. I didn't want to die. And so, the battle began.

Celebrating with John at my 60th birthday party. I was looking forward to a happy and healthy future, but the world had other plans.

That night, unable to sleep, I sat alone on the couch. The house was silent, the darkness almost oppressive. Yet in that stillness, clarity emerged. I thought about my upcoming 50th birthday, the milestones I hadn't yet reached – weddings, anniversaries, Christmases. I wasn't done with life. The determination to fight ignited within me. From that moment, I vowed to take it one day at a time. Each day became precious, a gift to cherish.

On the day of my surgery, fear gripped me as I lay on the gurney. The mention of nuclear dye tracing cancer near my lungs sent me spiralling into panic. "What if it's everywhere?" The uncertainty was crushing. When I woke up, pain and relief flooded my senses. The surgery had been a success – only a quarter of my right breast had been removed, and the cancer hadn't spread. Gratitude surged through me. But the journey was far from over. My surgeon recommended radiotherapy as a precaution and I resolved to do whatever it took to keep this intruder at bay. John, however, was hesitant. "Nilla, the cancer is gone. Why put yourself through this?" But my answer was firm: "Because I want to live."

The first day of radiotherapy was one of the hardest. John had flown to Vancouver to be with his son, Jason, leaving me to face the treatment with the support of a dear friend. As I entered the cold, clinical room, tears welled up. The sight of the lone treatment table under harsh lights was a stark reminder of my vulnerability. I felt utterly alone. But deep down, I knew this was my fight. No one could win this war for me.

A toast to a bright future on board our river cruise from Budapest to Amsterdam.

As treatment progressed, I unknowingly found myself slipping into a dark place. Depression was slowly creeping in, uninvited and insidious. I cried constantly, feeling like a shadow of my former self. My relationships strained under the weight of my emotions, and even John, my rock, seemed distant. It was a breast cancer survivor who gently warned me, "Be mindful not to let depression take hold." Her words struck a chord, so I was determined not to let that happen. However, without realising it, I had been sinking.

During this time, I lived in Perth with my baby brother, Gian Carlo and his partner Maria, who were both incredibly supportive. Though their kindness was constant, I often felt overwhelmed by the isolation and weight of my emotions. The helplessness of depression seemed to consume me. But every evening, I cooked them a meal.

Cooking wasn't just about feeding them – it became my anchor. It was my way of thanking them for their kindness, but more importantly, it was my way of reconnecting with myself and the world around me. When everything else felt out of my control, cooking was something I could hold onto, something that gave me purpose. Each dish I prepared was a small act of love, a gesture that transcended words.

Food became my therapy. It didn't cure what I was going through, but it allowed me to nurture those around me while nurturing myself. Through food, I found solace in the rhythm of chopping, stirring, and serving. I began to realise that in these small moments of giving, I was slowly healing. Cooking helped me feel grounded, connected, and, in a way, more alive.

A turning point came in February 2006. John sent me an email – a lifeline disguised as a suggestion. It proposed attending a personal development seminar. I was shocked. We were living in the same house, yet he chose email over a conversation. The realisation of how far we had drifted hit me like a freight train. Still, I responded with a resounding yes.

That seminar was transformative. Over the course of two days, I rediscovered my strength. I learned that I held the power to shape my life, to heal, and to thrive. The experience was far more than just an inspiring weekend – it marked the beginning of a profound transformation. But John didn't stop there. He gifted me the entire course they were offering, which took five months to complete, and in doing so, he gave me the gift of believing in myself when I had lost all belief. His gift was not just about the seminar; it was a belief in me, in my potential, and in my ability to rise above the challenges I faced.

Cheers to life with a glass of limoncello with freshly made Ricotta tart.

The course, with its challenges and breakthroughs, became the foundation for the life I am living today. It was life-changing, life-defining. Each lesson, each exercise, each moment of reflection built on the last, leading me to a place of clarity and strength I had never known before. I learned to trust myself again, to step into my power, and to release the fear and doubt that had held me captive for far too long.

Without that course, without John's unwavering belief in me, I truly believe I wouldn't be here now. It wasn't just about gaining knowledge – it was about learning to heal, to rise, and to step into the life I had always dreamed of. What I gained from that experience went far beyond practical tools; it gave me the courage to rebuild myself from the inside out. It gave

All dolled up and cuddled up for the wedding of Tim and Amy Stockdale - our family friends.

John and I sailing through life with each other's love and support.

me the strength to see that I am worthy of the life I desire and the power to create it.

John's belief in me wasn't just a gentle encouragement – it was a steadfast, unwavering faith in who I could become. His gift was the catalyst that sparked this transformation, but it was his belief in my potential that fuelled my journey. With every challenge I faced, his love and support were the bedrock that kept me grounded. In return, I learned to believe in myself, to trust the process and to keep moving forward – no matter what. His gift was a reminder that sometimes, the most precious thing we can give someone is not just a material possession, but the belief in their ability to rise.

John did another amazing thing while I was away from home for treatment. Completely unbeknown to me, he arranged for a renovation which completely moved the kitchen – MY kitchen! Various friends and family members have used words such as "brave" and "completely insane" to describe someone mad enough to renovate a kitchen without first running the idea by his wife. After all, this was the Daniele family home – the home my Papa built. It could have all ended terribly. Instead, what I came home to discover was a renovation that was handled expertly and with a sympathetic eye to my heritage and a vision for the future.

The arched brickwork over what was once Papa's bar and glassware shelves was transformed into a type of crypt containing a shelf using timber from a Norfolk Island pine tree in the yard which my Mama had planted. There was a new walk-in pantry and oven and cabinetry but – most curious of all – a massive island bench was installed that would comfortably seat 12 people. Why on earth would John build such a thing in a house with only two people living in it? Clearly, he already had in his mind that if a thing such as classes at "Nilla's Italian Kitchen" was to be invented, it

A September 2024 ravioli class looking forward to enjoying the fruits of their labours.

would require the right kitchen. I suspect it was a case of him waiting for me to catch up and arrive at the realisation of what needed to be done. Either way, it is a space that I dearly love and I particularly appreciate that it is a sanctuary that I have used to touch so many lives by sharing the gifts I've been given.

The experience of breast cancer reshaped my life. It taught me that challenges, no matter how daunting, carry the seeds of growth and transformation. Today, I live with gratitude – for John, for my health and for the ability to inspire others.

Breast cancer wasn't a death sentence for me; it was a life sentence – a call to live fully, without fear or regret. And every day, I honour that call by embracing my passion and purpose, by cherishing the miracle of love that saw me through the darkest of times.

If something quietly stirred or stayed with you, there's a world beyond these pages where kindred hearts gather. Visit kneadinghope.com.au/stirred when it feels right.

John and Nonna Nilla cooking with Harvey.

It was all hands on deck for this class in 2024.

My idea of heaven - at work with an armful of pasta in our wonderful kitchen.

Chilli Con Carne

DURING my treatment and while living with my little brother and his partner, cooking meals like this chilli con carne became a way for me to stay connected to myself and my loved ones. Despite the heaviness of the situation, there was something about cooking that brought comfort – not just to them, but to me as well. Preparing this dish and sharing it with them was my way of thanking them for their support and showing love in the only way I could during that time. Much like the layers of flavours in chilli con carne, my journey through treatment was complex – each step, each challenge, added a new layer to the healing process. The heat of the chilli and the depth of the spices reflected the intensity of my emotions, while the slow simmering allowed everything to come together, just as time and care helped me find my balance again. In the end, it wasn't just about the food; it was about the way the ingredients – like love, patience, and resilience – could blend together to create something nourishing, something that could feed both the body and the soul.

INGREDIENTS:
- 500g ground beef (or a mix of beef and pork)
- 1 large onion, finely chopped
- 2 cloves garlic, minced
- 1 red capsicum, diced
- 1 green capsicum, diced
- 1 can (400g) diced tomatoes
- 1 can (400g) kidney beans, drained and rinsed
- 1 can (400g) black beans, drained and rinsed
- 1 tablespoon tomato paste
- 2 tablespoons chilli powder (adjust to taste)
- 1 teaspoon ground cumin
- 1 teaspoon smoked paprika
- 1/2 teaspoon ground cinnamon
- 1-2 fresh red **chillies** (optional, for extra heat)
- 1 cup beef or vegetable broth
- Salt and pepper to taste
- Olive oil for cooking
- Fresh coriander for garnish (optional)
- Sour cream and shredded cheese (optional, for serving)

METHOD:
- Heat a little olive oil over medium heat, add the ground meat and cook until browned, breaking it up into small pieces with a spoon. Once browned, remove excess fat if needed.
- Add the chopped onion, garlic and bell peppers to the pot. Cook for about 5 minutes, stirring occasionally until softened.
- Stir in the chilli powder, cumin, smoked paprika and cinnamon. If using fresh chillies, chop them finely and add them in at this point. Cook for 2 minutes, allowing the spices to bloom and release their aroma.
- Add the tomato paste and stir it through the mixture before adding the diced tomatoes, kidney beans, black beans and broth. Stir everything together until well combined.
- Bring the mixture to a simmer and reduce the heat to low. Let it cook for at least 30 minutes, stirring occasionally, until thickened. If you prefer a spicier chilli, add more chilli powder or fresh chillies at this point.
- Season with salt and pepper to taste.
- Ladle the chilli into bowls and garnish with fresh coriander, sour cream, and shredded cheese if desired.

A soul-soothing bowl of chilli con carne.

CHAPTER 6

Lost to the Dark Side: A Journey Through Light and Shadow

A life that once shone brightly, now scattered like rabbits in the dark – fleeting yet unforgettable. In the silence of his absence, only memories remain, along with a recipe that speaks of the man he could have been before the darkness consumed him.

Cesare as a cheeky young boy.

MY brother Cesare was always a complicated soul, brimming with talent, charm, and an infectious zest for life. He was the kind of person who could light up a room with a joke, spin you around the dance floor until you forgot the world, and then leave you marvelling at his intelligence during a late-night conversation. But those gifts came with shadows.

His charm became a mask for deception, his wit a deflection from responsibility, and his appetite for life an addiction to chaos. Over the years, his choices fractured relationships and led him far from the brother I once knew. From Europe, Belize to the Philippines, the stories of his missteps became darker, more desperate, and harder to reconcile with the person I still loved.

Addiction, as I came to learn, doesn't just steal from the addict; it robs everyone who loves them. It is a slow, painful erosion, a gradual death of dreams. While Cesare spiralled deeper into his drug-infused life, those of us left behind held onto pieces of him, watching him slip further away, feeling powerless and heartbroken. The endless cycle of hope and disappointment, the endless promises of change followed by devastating falls, was a torment I wouldn't wish on anyone.

In 2009, my brother reached out from a prison in Belize, a cry for help wrapped in an email full of regret and promises. He spoke of a newfound clarity, of prayer and repentance, of longing to return to his family and right his wrongs. I responded with love but also with boundaries, unable to offer financial help but holding onto a sliver of hope that he could turn his life around.

But hope is a fragile thing. Over the years, thousands of dollars and countless hours were spent trying to help him find his footing. Each time, I prayed it would be the last time I would have to fund him, that this time he would change. Yet the pattern repeated – a brief moment of redemption followed by another fall. In 2016, when the Department of Foreign Affairs and Trade called to tell me he had been arrested again, this time in the Philippines, I felt something inside me break.

For my own health and sanity, I made the impossible decision to cut off contact. Blocking his messages and refusing to take his calls felt like betrayal, but it was also an act of self-preservation. I cried for hours, grieving not only for the brother I had lost to addiction and poor choices but for the brother I would never have again.

I can just hear Cesare saying, "Salute e buon apetito!"

Once I had told my little brother, Gian Carlo, what had happened, he stepped in where I left off. His words to me were, "Nilla, you shouldn't have had to do this on your own. I will deal with this from now on", but the weight of my Cesare's struggles proved too much for anyone to carry. Five months later, he died of a heart attack on the way to the hospital – a prisoner in both body and soul.

The loss was profound, not only because of his death but because of the years we had already lost to the dark side of life. Cesare's absence is a void that will never truly heal, a reminder of what addiction and despair can steal from a family. We all saw his potential – the brilliance, the kindness, the joy – but addiction suffocated it, leaving us to mourn the person he could have been. It's a grief that lingers, a grief for both the person lost and the version of them that never had the chance to flourish.

Yet amidst the sorrow, I try to remember the brighter moments: his laugh, his generosity, the times he brought joy before his world grew too heavy. On one of the rare occasions that we managed to be in contact, Cesare, in a moment of clarity, gave me a recipe for rabbit. The irony of it now isn't lost on me – much like the elusive rabbit that dashes and hides, my brother had disappeared into his drug-infused life, scattering himself across the globe in search of solace he couldn't find.

The recipe he gave me was simple but flavourful, a reflection of his charm that could still sneak through at times. Yet, it also mirrored his life – a recipe that required time and patience, yet always had an element of unpredictability. I've made the dish since, and with each bite, I am reminded of the person my brother was before the darkness took over – someone who could still share something beautiful, even if it was fleeting, like a rabbit.

After Cesare's passing, a group of his overseas friends created a page on Facebook, called "In Memory of Cesare Fermino Daniele". It was here, in the shared memories of friends that I learned even more about the man he had been. Among the posts, one stood out and stayed with me. It was from someone who had known him back when he was vibrant and full of life—long before the chaos took hold.

"Ces bounced into my life in 2002 at the Leoniki. He was my rep and signed me up into the world of Club Greece. Since that day, we became firm friends. I owe Ces a great deal. Because of him, I met some of my best friends, have the happiest memories, and learned a lot from him. Ces always made me laugh – even in our darkest times. He was a whirlwind, always positive, determined, intelligent, happy with a bit of crazy thrown in. He may have made some bad decisions, but he never blamed anyone but himself. He picked himself up, dusted himself off, and kept on trying. His strength and determination were inspirational. His goal was always to make his daughters proud and to return to his family when he felt he had achieved that for them."

Those words cut deep, reaffirming the strength of Cesare's character before the darkness overtook him. They spoke to the essence of who he had been – strong, positive, and determined to do right by his family. I reflected on the times when we had been together, making dinner and sharing stories. He had a gift for bringing joy to the simplest of moments, and his culinary skills had never failed to impress.

Cesare was a self-made chef, not just by trade, but by passion. His food was an extension of his heart, and each meal he prepared was a reflection of the love he had, even if he could never fully show it in his life.

"Cesare, you were a legend. They broke the mould when they made you. I hope your family finds strength and comfort from the love your friends and those who knew you have for you. You had a big heart, a good heart, and you were loved by all who were lucky enough to know you. God bless you, Ces. I hope you finally have peace. I will miss you so much. A month ago, you told me life was full of surprises. Well, this is one neither of us could have ever seen coming. Thank you, Ces. Goodnight, my friend. Sweet dreams."

Through these memories, the anger and sorrow began to shift, slowly transforming into something more profound: gratitude. Gratitude for the man Cesare had been, for the bond we shared in better times, and for the lessons he unknowingly taught me, even as I struggled to understand the decisions he made. Cesare's life, like that of a rabbit, was a journey between light and shadow – hopping from one fleeting moment of brightness to the next, always running, always searching, but never truly finding peace. Despite the darkness that enveloped him, his light would occasionally break through

– sometimes in moments of laughter, sometimes in the meals he lovingly prepared, and in the quiet moments when I knew, deep down, that he loved his family, even though his addiction kept him at a distance. The love he carried for us was only truly known to him, hidden in the layers of pain and chaos, but it was there, buried beneath the weight of his struggles.

When Cesare passed, his ashes were brought back to Albany, where he now rests alongside my Mama and Papa. In the same place where our family's roots run deep, Cesare is laid to rest, the final chapter of a life marked by love, loss and the silent search for peace. I like to think that, in the end, he found some measure of solace in being back with his family, even if it was too late to heal the rift caused between us by his addiction.

Now, every time I prepare the rabbit recipe he gave me, I feel the weight of his absence in a different way. I reflect on the vibrant man he once was, the brother I will forever carry in my heart and the love he struggled to show. Each time I make this dish, I honour the joy and the pain of having had him in my life, and I remember that despite everything, Cesare's spirit will always be with me – carried in the meals we shared, the laughter we had, and the love that I know he held for us, even when the darkness took him.

Each time I read this I think of my little brother.

If something quietly stirred or stayed with you, there's a world beyond these pages where kindred hearts gather. Visit kneadinghope.com.au/stirred when it feels right.

Cesare's Legacy on a Plate – Rabbit in White Wine

CESARE'S life was a constant dance between light and shadow, much like a rabbit darting between the darkness and the fleeting warmth of the sun. His days were filled with moments of brilliance and darkness, always searching for peace, but often caught in the turmoil of his own battles. His was a life of paradox: tender yet wild, simple yet rich, struggling to escape the weight of his choices but always yearning for connection.

This dish, a gift from Cesare, is more than just a recipe – it's a reflection of his spirit. Like him, it's humble and simple on the surface, yet deep and rich with complexity. Every time I prepare it, I'm reminded of the brother I lost, of the joy and pain he carried, and the love he gave in his own way. In each bite, I honour both the light and shadow of his life, keeping his memory alive with every flavour, every moment shared.

INGREDIENTS:

- 1 whole rabbit, cut into serving pieces
- 2 tablespoons olive oil
- 2 onions, finely chopped
- 4 garlic cloves, minced
- 2 carrots, sliced
- 2 celery stalks, chopped
- 1 cup white wine
- 2 cups chicken stock
- 1 teaspoon rosemary, chopped
- 1 teaspoon thyme, chopped
- Salt and pepper to taste
- Fresh parsley, chopped (for garnish)

METHOD:

- In a large pot, heat olive oil over medium heat. Add rabbit pieces and brown on all sides, then remove from the pot and set aside.
- In the same pot, add onions, garlic, carrots, and celery. Sauté until softened.
- Pour in the white wine, scraping the bottom of the pot to release any browned bits. Let it simmer for a couple of minutes.
- Return the rabbit pieces to the pot, add chicken stock, rosemary, thyme, salt, and pepper. Bring to a boil, then reduce heat and let simmer for 1 to 1.5 hours, or until the rabbit is tender.
- Garnish with fresh parsley and serve with crusty bread or roasted potatoes.

The delicious rabbit is ready.

CHAPTER 7

The Camino and the Worn Path: A Journey from Struggle to Strength

The Camino de Santiago: A journey of pain, healing, and rediscovery, where each step became a prayer for strength, resilience and renewal.

THE Camino de Santiago is often called a journey of transformation and, for me, it became a raw, unflinching mirror of life's twists, turns, and the unexpected challenges we face. What began as an adventure in September 2016, walking from León to Santiago with my best friend, Jeanette, evolved into something much deeper – both physically demanding and emotionally awakening. As each step stretched into another, it became not just a journey across Spain, but a journey into the heart of my own soul.

This path unfolded across three stages: my first Camino, and the second and final ones walked with my husband, John. The first was an experience of new beginnings. However, as I stepped into the final two Caminos with John by my side, I soon realised I was facing more than just the pilgrimage itself. The weight of my body's resistance, the increasing pain and the limitations of my physical form became a constant companion, as each Camino slowly pushed me further into a space I had never known – into a space where endurance became a battle not just for the body, but for my spirit.

I am so grateful for what the Camino taught me.

The pain that once seemed bearable soon became unbearable, a reminder of my body's limits. What had begun as an inspiring challenge soon turned into a fight for survival. These final stages of the Camino did not just challenge my body – they tested the very essence of my strength. Every step felt like an uphill battle, where the world around me blurred, but my determination and willpower remained the only things that kept me moving forward.

The first leg of my pilgrimage took me 300 kilometres from León to Santiago. In the heat of the Spanish sun and the steep climbs into the mountains, every step seemed to demand something deeper from me. I've always been a slow walker by nature, and with the weight of my past, including my breast cancer battle, it felt like my body was dragging me along, unwillingly. Yet, even as my legs ached, my heart heavy with memories, I reminded myself that I was walking not just for me but for those who could no longer make this journey.

Day 2 of that first Camino remains etched in my memory, as if it were a painting hung in my heart. The scorching Spanish sun beat down mercilessly, its heat wrapping around me like a thick, suffocating blanket. The 21 kilometres from Astorga to Rabanal felt endless, each step an act of defiance against the exhaustion that seemed to cling to my every movement. The path, winding and relentless, mirrored the struggles I'd been carrying inside for years. The air was heavy, and with each step, the weight of my own burdens seemed to press down harder.

When we finally reached Cruz de Ferro, the iron cross that towers over the Camino, it felt as though the earth itself was holding its breath. It is here that pilgrims leave a stone at the foot of the cross – a symbol of shedding their burdens, of letting go. I paused, my heart full, my chest tight, as I placed my stone at the base of the cross. The tears I had held inside for so long finally broke free, flowing down my face without shame. I wasn't just grieving the loss of those I loved; I was grieving the years of struggle, of survival and of the quiet battles I had fought alone.

In that moment, I realised that I wasn't walking just for me. I was walking for everyone who could no longer walk. For every heart broken, for every soul lost, for every person who had been left behind. I was walking in their memory, carrying their pain and their hope with each step, honouring the journey they would never complete.

The long and winding road of the Camino.

Little did I know, though, that the greatest challenge I faced was yet to come. While I was focused on the emotional weight I was carrying, my body was quietly warning me that it, too, was nearing its limit. My hips, the very foundation that had carried me so far, were beginning to wear out, but I couldn't see it yet. I was still wrapped in the rush of the Camino's power, and it wasn't until much later that I would understand the physical toll this journey would exact from me.

The second leg of the journey, in 2017, was from St Jean Pied de Port to León. This Camino felt more personal, as it was shared with my husband John. We walked 580 kilometres together, but this time, the pain in my hips was becoming more than just a passing discomfort – it was a constant companion. By now, the pain had intensified, but I pressed on, thinking I could push through it, as I had done in the past.

This stage of the Camino tested my resolve and my relationship with John. My slow pace, fuelled by my determination to finish, caused frustration between John and me. Despite my internal struggles, I hid the truth from him and from myself – this journey wasn't just about reaching the end. It had become a test of endurance, both for my body and my soul. I wasn't walking just to walk. I was walking to prove something to myself.

By the time we embarked on our third and final Camino from Porto to Santiago in 2018, the pain in my hips was unbearable. Every step felt like I was walking on fire, yet I continued, believing that the completion of the Camino would somehow bring peace. It was during this final leg that I had no choice but to face the truth – I couldn't keep pushing my body beyond its limits.

Nilla and John on the Camino.

At this point, my physical condition had deteriorated significantly. What had once been a minor inconvenience in my hips had become a debilitating issue, forcing me to slow down even further. I was barely able to make it through the days, and each night, I collapsed in pain, knowing I was nearing the end of my journey, not just on the Camino but with my ability to move freely.

Looking back, I realise that my stubbornness had kept me going, but it was also my undoing. My body had been telling me to stop, but I refused to listen. It wasn't until I finally sought medical help that I discovered the extent of the damage: severe osteoarthritis, bone-on-bone contact, and spurs that had been silently growing for years. The X-ray results confirmed it – the only solution was surgery, both hips needed to be replaced.

The realisation was devastating: my body, which had carried me so far, was now the very thing holding me back. The Camino had pushed me beyond my limits, yet it was also showing me a profound truth – that healing, like walking, requires acceptance of where we are, not just where we wish to be.

The days leading up to surgery were filled with uncertainty and fear. Losing my mobility felt like losing a part of myself. I had walked hundreds of kilometres across Spain and Portugal with pain, but now, I was faced with the reality of not being able to walk at all. The very independence I had cherished was slipping away. I went from walking through villages and mountains to relying on crutches and walkers for basic tasks.

But even in this vulnerability, I found strength. The lessons of the Camino, lessons of perseverance and patience, guided me through this new chapter. Each step of the recovery journey was a reminder that healing takes time, and it is only through acceptance and small steps that progress is made. Through physical therapy, I re-learned how to walk. And every time I took a step I reminded myself that healing was a journey – just like the Camino itself.

Today, I am walking again – not just with my legs, but with a renewed sense of gratitude for the simple act of movement. What once felt like a struggle is now a celebration. The Camino de Santiago may have helped to wear out my hips, but it also prepared me for the journey of recovery. Each step on that sacred path taught me something that I now carry into my everyday life: that no matter how heavy the burden, there is always a way forward.

The Camino was the first stage of a much bigger journey – one that continues to unfold. It taught me about resilience, patience, and the power of accepting our limitations. And just as the Camino helped me find strength in walking, I am now finding strength in each small step I take on the path of recovery.

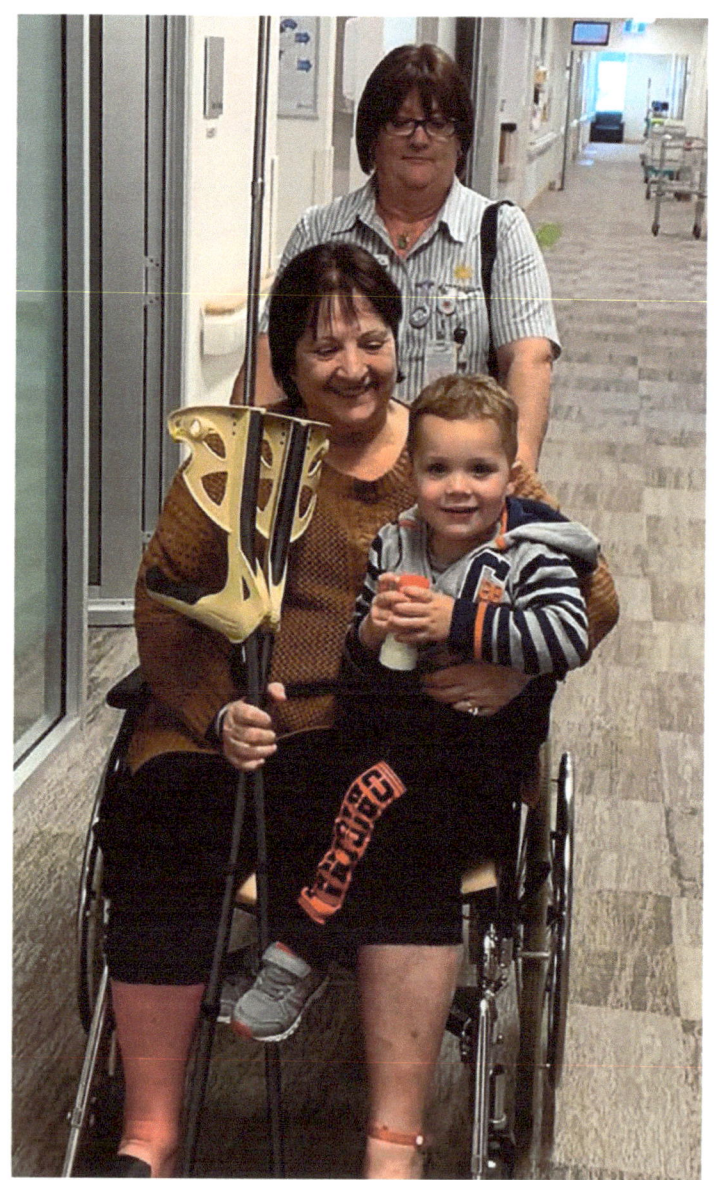

Leaving hospital with Harvey, my second hip replaced and ready to take on the world.

If something quietly stirred or stayed with you, there's a world beyond these pages where kindred hearts gather. Visit kneadinghope.com.au/stirred when it feels right.

Torta di Santiago

THE simplest of ingredients makes the most delicious torta! In many ways, the Torta di Santiago, a traditional Spanish almond cake from Santiago de Compostela, embodies the spirit of the Camino: simple yet full of depth, rich in history and meaning. This cake is often enjoyed after a long walk, symbolising the completion of a journey. Just as the Torta di Santiago requires patience, precision, and time, so too does healing – one ingredient, one moment, one step at a time. This Torta di Santiago is more than just a dessert – it's a reminder of the journey I have walked, and continue to walk. Just as the ingredients blend together to create something greater than the sum of their parts, my journey has blended pain, perseverance and triumph. Each step on the Camino taught me patience, and each bite of this cake, like the lessons I've learned, carries a sweet reminder that no matter the struggles we face, there is always a way forward.

INGREDIENTS:

- 250g ground almonds
- 200g sugar
- 4 large eggs
- 1 tbsp lemon zest
- 1 tsp ground cinnamon
- 1/2 teaspoon baking powder
- Pinch of salt
- Powdered sugar for dusting
- A cross template (optional)

Arriving at the Cathedral of Santiago de Compostela in Galicia, Spain, after walking the Camino is an experience I will never forget.

METHOD:

- Preheat oven to 180°C (350°F). Grease and line a 23 cm (9-inch) round cake pan.
- In a large bowl, whisk the eggs and sugar until pale and fluffy.
- Gently fold in the ground almonds, cinnamon, lemon zest, baking powder, and salt. Mix until well combined.
- Pour the batter into the prepared pan and smooth the top.
- Bake for 30-40 minutes, or until a toothpick comes out clean. Let the cake cool completely in the pan.
- Once cooled, place the cross template on top of the cake and dust generously with powdered sugar.
- Remove the template carefully, revealing the cross design.

A stencil for your *Tortia de Santiago*. The top of the pie is decorated with powdered sugar, stencilled by a silhouette of the Cross of Saint James (*cruz de Santiago*) which gives the pastry its name. The origin of the cross being decorated on the cake dates to 1924.

45

CHAPTER 8

Loss of Connection: A Business, A Family, A Heartbroken Change

Through loss comes transformation – finding new paths to nourish, reconnect, and heal.

THERE was a time, before the world changed so dramatically, when our travel agency wasn't just a business – it was a family. It wasn't simply about bookings, itineraries or commissions – it was about people. The faces of our clients were familiar, but not in the transactional sense. They weren't just names on a list. We had seen them through births, weddings, and anniversaries. We had mourned with them in their grief, celebrated their milestones, and shared in their dreams of far-off lands. It was a space where we didn't just help them plan their holidays. We walked beside them as part of their lives, woven into the fabric of their personal stories.

I loved every moment of it – not because it was a means of income, but because it was a place where hearts connected. Over the years, we poured love into our business, into our clients, and into each other. We hosted thank-you luncheons, special events, and gatherings – simple expressions of gratitude that reflected my passion for food as well as travel.

But those luncheons were never just about food. They were about the people sitting around the table, sharing their hopes, dreams, and the little joys of their lives with us. We didn't just serve a meal; we served connection, belonging and love. I watched as our clients gathered in the office, not just to plan their holidays, but to share a part of their lives with us. We were part of their most intimate moments—helping them plan a honeymoon, a retirement trip, a pilgrimage or just a getaway.

There was magic in the room when they sat down in front of us, their eyes sparkling with excitement as we brought their dreams to life. These weren't just transactions – they were relationships, nurtured and built over years. I was proud to be more than just a travel agent. I was part of their stories and part of their family. They were not just clients; they were people we deeply cared about.

When the pandemic hit, it was like a dream shattered in an instant. The phones stopped ringing, the laughter that used to fill the office disappeared into silence and we closed the doors. The connections we had spent decades building suddenly felt fragile, like glass slipping from our hands.

What was once a hub of energy and life became an empty, hollow space. The smiles, the warmth, the stories – we no longer had the privilege of experiencing those in the same way. It wasn't just our livelihood that we lost; it was the heart of our business, the community and the family we had created – and our clients lost their dreams. I mourned the loss, but it wasn't just for the business. It was for the moments we shared, for the friendships formed over years of travel planning. The loss felt personal, deep and profound.

How do you quantify the loss of years spent building something that was not just a business but a sanctuary of connection? The travel agency had been our heartbeat for more than 40 years. It had sustained us. And suddenly, it was gone. The loss wasn't just in numbers; it was in the absence of the familiar faces, the routines we'd come to rely upon and the shared joy of serving others.

Our beloved Travel Agency once COVID stopped the world.

The world had changed, and in many ways, so had we. But it wasn't just the financial strain that caused the most pain – it was the absence of the community, the daily interactions, the sense of purpose that came from helping people create memories. The isolation was overwhelming. The pandemic stripped away what had been a fundamental part of our lives, leaving a void that was hard to fill.

But in the midst of the sorrow, I realised something powerful. While we may have lost the physical connection, the relationships, the essence of what we built, could never truly disappear. Just like the pasta dough I kneaded and shaped, the memories we created together, though tempered by time, are still being shaped by the warmth of those connections. In the end, it wasn't about the business – it was about the people, the love and the trust we had shared. It was about the spirit of the community we built.

Though the doors to the travel agency are closed, the heart of it lives on in the kitchen, in the meals I prepare and in the way I continue to connect with others. Those bonds may not have been forged over itineraries and plane tickets, but they were built just the same – through trust, through love, and through the shared moments of life. Our agency may have closed, but the legacy of what we created – the people, the relationships and the memories – will never be forgotten. It lives in the food I make, the laughter shared in my cooking classes and in the community I now have – not as clients, but as family.

One such meal I hold close to my heart is cannelloni – a dish passed down through the years, rich with memories and love, just like the ones we built together. Cannelloni has always been a way to share my passion for food with those I love.

If something quietly stirred or stayed with you, there's a world beyond these pages where kindred hearts gather. Visit kneadinghope.com.au/stirred when it feels right.

Spinach & Ricotta Cannelloni – Building New Beginnings

CANNELLONI, a dish filled with love, is a recipe that represents the heart of what I shared with my clients. Made with fresh pasta and a rich spinach and ricotta filling, it's not just food – it's a symbol of the care, time and attention we poured into our relationships. This dish, though simple, carries deeper meaning – connection, love and gratitude. Now, as I share these recipes in this new chapter of my life, I'm reminded that the true treasures are the bonds we create through food, travel and shared experiences. Though the agency is gone, the love we shared through meals will live on. In its layers, I see the layers of life – each ingredient, each step, each small effort that comes together to create something beautiful. And much like the connections we made with those we served, each rolled tube is a reminder that what we build with care, attention and love – though tested by time – never truly disappears.

INGREDIENTS FOR FRESH PASTA:
- 2 1/2 cups all-purpose flour (plus extra for dusting)
- 3 large eggs
- 1 tablespoon olive oil
- 1/2 teaspoon salt

INGREDIENTS FOR THE FILLING:
- 500g (17.6oz) ricotta cheese
- 300g (10.5oz) fresh spinach (or frozen, thawed and drained)
- 1/4 cup grated Parmesan cheese
- 1/2 teaspoon ground nutmeg
- Salt and pepper to taste
- 1 egg, lightly beaten

INGREDIENTS FOR THE SAUCE:
- 700g (24oz) tomato passata (or crushed tomatoes)
- 1 onion, finely chopped
- 2 garlic cloves, minced
- 2 tablespoons olive oil
- A pinch of sugar (optional)
- Salt and pepper to taste
- Fresh basil, to garnish

METHOD:
- Prepare the fresh pasta: On a clean work surface, mound the flour and make a well in the centre. Crack the eggs into the well and add the olive oil and salt. Slowly incorporate the flour into the eggs until the dough begins to come together. Knead for about 10 minutes until smooth and elastic. Cover with plastic wrap and let it rest for at least 30 minutes.
- Prepare the filling: In a large bowl, combine the ricotta, spinach, Parmesan, nutmeg and a pinch of salt and pepper. Stir in the beaten egg to bind the filling. Set aside.
- Roll out the pasta: Divide the dough into four pieces. Roll each piece out on a floured surface or pasta machine to about 3mm (1/8 inch) thickness. Cut the rolled dough into sheets large enough to wrap around your filling – about 8cm (3 inches) wide.

Each roll of cannelloni is filled with love and goodness!

• Fill the pasta: Spoon a generous amount of the spinach and ricotta filling onto the centre of each pasta sheet. Carefully roll up the pasta sheets, encasing the filling inside.

• Prepare the sauce: Heat olive oil in a large saucepan over medium heat. Add the onion and garlic and sauté until soft. Stir in the passata, salt, pepper and a pinch of sugar if needed to balance the acidity. Let simmer for about 15-20 minutes.

• Assemble and bake: Preheat your oven to 180°C (350°F). Spread a layer of tomato sauce on the bottom of a baking dish. Place the filled pasta rolls on top of the sauce and cover with the remaining sauce. Top with grated mozzarella and parmesan. Cover with foil and bake for 25 minutes, then remove the foil and bake for another 10 minutes until the cheese is melted and golden.

• Serve: Garnish with fresh basil leaves and serve hot, sharing with those you cherish.

49

CHAPTER 9

A New Chapter: From Silence to Strength

In the quiet moments of uncertainty, we rise – one small step, one tender knead, one hopeful breath at a time.

I learned that the quiet time spent preparing dough brought a deep sense of peace and connectivity.

THE world, as we knew it, changed overnight with the pandemic of 2020. One moment, the doors of possibility were wide open – inviting conversations, laughter and human connection. And the next, they slammed shut. The faces I once greeted with a smile – the familiar faces of clients, friends and colleagues – became nothing more than pixels on a screen. The warmth of human touch, the comforting exchanges of shared moments and the everyday conversations that once filled our days were replaced with silence, isolation and the haunting uncertainty of a world turned upside down by this global crisis. It wasn't just a loss of business – it was the loss of the very fabric that had connected us all. The rhythm of life, the energy of community and the bonds we had worked so hard to build were all swept away in an instant. What followed was a sense of disconnection so profound, it reached into the core of who I was, leaving a gaping hole where connection once lived.

The days stretched on – weeks, months – each one blurring into the next. And in that vast, aching void, I realised something I wasn't prepared to face: the toll on my mental health was far greater than I had anticipated. Like so many others, I had spent my life rushing from one thing to the next, constantly giving and doing for others, always looking outward for validation, for meaning. But the pandemic forced me to look inward and, in that quiet, I came face-to-face with my own fragility.

I had been strong – resilient even – through the ups and downs, through the highs and lows of life. But now, in the silence of lockdown, I was unmoored. The identity I had built around work, around community, around being "needed", was now gone. I wasn't just mourning the loss of the travel agency; I was mourning the loss of connection, the loss of purpose and the loss of the life I once knew. And in the midst of that, I began to feel like I was losing myself.

But as the days passed, I found a strange form of solace in the simplest of acts. Baking. Specifically, sourdough bread. In the chaos of everything slipping through my fingers, there was a groundedness in kneading dough and in the act of patiently waiting for the yeast to rise. Sourdough bread, with its deep, slow fermentation process, became a metaphor for everything I was feeling – slow, uncertain, but with the promise of something nourishing at the end. The bread itself required time, patience and constant care. Just like me. At first, I failed – again and again. The dough wouldn't rise, the texture was off or the flavour too tangy. But I didn't stop. I kept going, day after day, mixing, kneading and letting time do its work. With every failed attempt, I learned. With every mistake, I discovered something new. And in that repetitive, therapeutic motion of kneading, I began to find small moments of peace.

But it wasn't just the dough that was rising. So was I. The lockdown, as isolating as it was, gave me the chance to rediscover something I hadn't realised I had lost: my own sense of inner strength. I had always prided myself on being resilient, on pushing through challenges, but this time, it wasn't about pushing through. It was about trusting the process – about allowing myself to rise, just as the dough did, in its own time and at its own pace.

The same patience I was learning in the kitchen became a guiding force for my mental health. In the quiet moments spent waiting for the dough to rise, I began to reflect on my own healing. And though it felt impossible at times, I began to believe that, like sourdough, I could rise again – stronger, more nourished and more resilient than before.

The pandemic, while it isolated us physically, also revealed something else – new possibilities. With the distractions of everyday hustle and bustle stripped away, there was space to see things differently. I began to see new ways of doing things, new opportunities and new ways to connect. Like sourdough, life began to rise in unexpected ways.

And, amidst the mayhem, there was something even more beautiful. A sense of community, of people looking out for each other and of finding connection in the most unlikely places. Whether it was sharing a recipe, checking in with a friend over the phone or joining virtual cooking classes, the pandemic created a new kind of bond between people. We learned to support each other, not just from afar, but from the heart. The community I had once known in the travel agency transformed and, while we couldn't be physically together, we found new ways to be there for each other.

This time of forced slowing down was not easy. The isolation, the loss of connection and the constant uncertainty – all of it weighed heavily on my mental health. But there, in the quiet moments, I realised something profound: even when we feel like we are falling apart, the act of doing something with love – nurturing something, even something as simple as bread – helps us to rebuild, bit by bit. Just as sourdough requires care and patience to develop its full flavour, so too does life require time to heal, to evolve and to rise again. It's in this waiting, in this nurturing, that we find the strength to rise up from the darkest places.

As I continued to bake, the process became more than just about making bread. It was about giving myself permission to heal, to grow, and to trust that, in time, I too would rise again. It was in these moments, as the dough rose beneath my hands, that I began to find a sense of peace that had eluded me for so long.

The pandemic may have kept us apart physically, but it also gave us the opportunity to reconnect with ourselves. We were no longer rushing from one thing to the next, consumed by the endless pace of life. In this forced stillness, we were given the chance to slow down and reevaluate what truly matters. And in that slowing down, I discovered something essential: that we are capable of healing – of rising – even when we can't see the way forward. Through the sourdough, I learned that healing takes time. And it was in that patience, that quiet care, that I found my way back to myself. Just like the bread, I had to trust the process. And as I did, I discovered it was not just the dough that rose – it was me...

If something quietly stirred or stayed with you, there's a world beyond these pages where kindred hearts gather. Visit kneadinghope.com.au/stirred when it feels right.

Sourdough Bread – Rising Stronger, One Step at a Time

HERE'S the recipe that helped me rise from the uncertainty of those months. Sourdough is more than just a recipe – it's a metaphor for how life works. The process requires time, attention and patience and, in the end, it results in something nourishing and beautiful. As I made this sourdough, I realised that it mirrored my own journey – waiting, kneading, rising. It reminded me that the most beautiful things take time to manifest. The process isn't always easy, but it is always worth it. Like the dough, we must be patient with ourselves, allowing time to rise and develop.

INGREDIENTS FOR THE STARTER:
- 1/2 cup (120ml) water (room temperature)
- 1/2 cup (60g) flour (whole wheat or all-purpose)

INGREDIENTS FOR THE DOUGH:
- 1 cup (240ml) sourdough starter (fed and active)
- 1 1/2 cups (360ml) water (room temperature)
- 3 cups (360g) bread flour
- 1 teaspoon salt

METHOD FOR THE STARTER:
- Create the starter: In a bowl, combine the water and flour. Stir together until there are no lumps. Cover with a cloth and leave in a warm spot for 24 hours. Every 12 hours, feed the starter with another 1/4 cup flour and 1/4 cup water.
- After 5-7 days, the starter should have risen, bubbled, and developed a sour aroma. At this point, it is ready to use in your dough.

METHOD FOR THE DOUGH:
- Mix the dough: In a large mixing bowl, combine the starter, water and flour. Stir to combine. Let rest for 30 minutes to 1 hour. (This is called autolyse).
- Knead the dough: After resting, add salt to the dough and knead for 10-15 minutes until smooth and elastic. If needed, add more flour to keep it from sticking.
- Bulk fermentation: Place the dough in a lightly oiled bowl and cover with a damp cloth. Let it rise for 4-6 hours, folding the dough every hour for the first 3 hours.
- Shape and proof: Shape the dough into a round or oval loaf. Place it in a well-floured proofing basket or bowl. Let the dough rest for 1-2 hours.

Sourdough Bread just out of the oven.

• Bake the bread: Preheat your oven to 450°F (230°C). Place a Dutch oven or baking pot with a lid inside to heat up. When ready, place your dough inside the hot pot, cover with the lid, and bake for 30 minutes. Then, uncover and bake for another 15 minutes until golden brown.

CHAPTER 10

Rising Through the Struggles: The Power of Transformation

**From pain to power, from struggle to strength –
together, we rise with hope.**

SOMETIMES, the deepest, most transformative journeys aren't the ones we choose. They're the ones life forces upon us. Life has a way of breaking us down, reshaping us in ways we never anticipated – forcing us to confront our greatest fears, our losses and our weaknesses. And yet, in those moments of devastation, something incredible happens: we find strength we didn't know we had. We rise, not just to survive, but to soar.

In every single wound, in every scar that time heals, there is a lesson, a message that says: you are capable of more than you think. The pain that once threatened to bury me, to drown me, is the same pain that now fuels the fire within me. It's a fire that burns brighter each day, guiding me, pushing me to reach higher and to create something bigger than myself. It's the fire of hope.

What is hope, if not the courage to keep moving forward, one step at a time, even when the way seems uncertain and when the end is not in sight? Hope is the spark that lights the path in the darkest of times. It's the heartbeat of resilience, the voice that whispers, "keep going", even when everything inside you screams to stop.

Deep in thought - there's something therapeutic about the quiet time spent on a mindful task like baking.

I've walked through darkness. I've faced the unbearable weight of loss. I've been brought to my knees by illness, by heartache, by the very things that should have broken me. But they didn't. And that's because in the ashes of despair, I learned the art of rising.

There were days when it felt impossible. Days when it seemed like I was stuck in an endless loop of failure, where my past mistakes, regrets, and pain threatened to define me. But there's something beautiful about hitting rock bottom. It forces you to look up, to ask yourself, "Is this where I want to stay?" And I didn't want to stay there.

54

I didn't want to remain in the place where the world felt dark, where I couldn't see a way forward. So, I started to ask questions that brought me to the surface. What if the pain I've endured has a purpose? What if everything I've been through is leading me to something greater? I started to see that the hardest moments in life are not meant to break us – they are meant to build us, to shape us into the people we are meant to become.

What I discovered is that hope doesn't live in the absence of hardship – it lives in the presence of resilience, in the quiet, consistent choice to keep going, even when everything inside you tells you to quit. Hope is not a fleeting emotion; it is a foundation. It is built on the small, everyday decisions to take one more step, to breathe through the pain, to let the light in, even when the storm is raging outside.

And I am here today, stronger and more grateful than ever before, not because life has been easy, but because I chose to embrace the power of hope and the power of transformation. Every setback has been an opportunity for a comeback. Every loss has been the foundation for a new beginning. Every tear has watered the soil from which my resilience grows.

As I look around me, I see people who have weathered their own storms. I see a community of warriors who have chosen to rise, chosen to step into their power, chosen to live with hope at the forefront of their lives. And I know, without a doubt, that we are capable of more than we ever believed possible.

Hope isn't a passive feeling; it's a call to action. It's about looking at the life you're living now and asking, "How can I transform this? How can I use what I've learned, what I've endured, to create something greater, not just for myself, but for the world around me?"

And that's why we are here, together, on this journey. We are a community bound by a common purpose: to transform our pain into power, our fear into courage, our uncertainty into certainty. We are here not just to survive, but to thrive.

I have walked the hardest roads. I have lived the hardest lessons. And now, I am sharing those lessons with you, because I know, deep in my soul, that you, too, have the

Taking time to stop and smell the truffles.

strength to rise. No matter where you've been, no matter what you've faced, there is a place for you in this community. We are stronger together. And together, we will rise higher than we ever thought possible.

So, if you're reading this and you're feeling lost, or unsure, or overwhelmed, take a deep breath and remember hope lives within you. It always has. It always will. You are not defined by your struggles; you are defined by the way you rise from them. I invite you to join us. To join a community of dreamers, doers and believers who know that no matter what we face, we are capable of more. Together, we will build something greater. Together, we will move from pain to power, from darkness to light, and we will inspire the world with the legacy of hope that we create together.

In the kitchen, kneading dough is a practice of patience, of working through resistance and of shaping something raw into something beautiful. Much like life, the process is not always easy, but with every fold and press, you create something stronger. Kneading Hope is about shaping the very fabric of our existence, just as we shape the dough – slowly, patiently and with intention. It's the lesson that no matter how difficult the process may be, you have the power to transform, to rise and to create something greater than you ever imagined.

Uncertainty, painful losses and physical challenges have helped shape the person I am today – and I am grateful for the lessons life has taught me.

Just as dough is kneaded, shaped and allowed to rise, our hopes and dreams are nurtured through the trials of life, the struggle, and the perseverance. In the kitchen, we learn that every ingredient, every moment of patience, and every act of love contributes to the final creation. And that is how we shape our lives – one step, one choice, one act of love at a time.

Through everything I've endured – the loss, the heartache, the pain – there is one truth I hold close: I have been shaped by all of it. I have risen, not in spite of my struggles, but because of them. Every moment of uncertainty, every challenge I faced, has become part of the dough that made me who I am today.

There were times I wanted to give up. Times when the weight of grief and loss felt unbearable. I would look at the empty spaces, at what was once whole, and feel the ache of what was missing. But then, just as dough needs to be worked and folded before it rises, I too had to fold myself back together. The love, the pain and the moments of silence – each one kneaded me into something new, something stronger.

The beauty of life is that just as dough rises, so do we. Each time I stumbled, each time I faced the darkness, I found that in my lowest moments, there was always something within me, a spark, a hope, that would rise. And just as bread is nurtured through time and patience, so too is the hope within us. The process of becoming, of truly rising to who we are meant to be, is never instant. It requires time, patience and the trust that no matter how many times we fall, we can rise again—stronger, more resilient and more filled with love and hope than before.

Through the pandemic, through the trials of uncertainty, we were all forced to slow down. The world stopped, but in the quiet stillness, we found that we were not powerless. Just like the bread dough, we had the ability to rise again. The act of kneading, of turning those humble ingredients into something beautiful, became a powerful metaphor for the journey I had been on. I could knead my hopes and dreams, my pains and losses, into something meaningful. I could rise – again, and again and again.

The pandemic, while keeping us physically apart, gave us the chance to reconnect with ourselves, to rediscover our resilience, and to find new ways of living. Through sourdough bread and simple acts of care, I found a renewed sense of purpose. I learned that it wasn't about the things I had lost, but about the things I could still create. In every loaf of bread, in every moment of patience, I saw that life was not something to be merely endured; it was something to be nurtured, just as dough is nurtured through its rises and falls.

As I look back on my journey, I realise that the most important lesson I've learned is that hope is not passive. Hope is something we actively knead into our lives. We choose it every day. We choose to rise, to grow, and to transform. Every challenge, every hardship, is an opportunity to knead more hope into the dough of our lives, shaping ourselves into something greater than we ever thought possible. I have risen, and I will rise again. And so will you. Together, we can knead hope into the very core of our lives and create a legacy of love, resilience and strength.

The act of mixing, kneading and shaping ingredients into something beautiful is a metaphor for the journey of life.

If something quietly stirred or stayed with you, there's a world beyond these pages where kindred hearts gather. Visit kneadinghope.com.au/stirred when it feels right.

Limoncello Tiramisu – Sweetness Born from Life's Challenges

MUCH like the life I've lived, this limoncello tiramisu holds both bitterness and sweetness in harmony. The limoncello – sharp, intense and with a bite – is a reminder of life's challenges, the struggles that shape us, the lessons we learn through pain. The Limoncello, bright and zesty, mirrors those moments of clarity, when a burst of hope cuts through the fog of uncertainty, reminding us that even in the darkest times, there is sweetness to be found.

The sweetness gives us the unexpected gifts of life like the love, the friendships and the moments of joy. The mascarpone cream, soft and delicate, embodies the resilience we develop over time and the strength that comes from choosing to rise, again and again. It is the softness we find when we accept our own vulnerabilities, the kindness we offer to others and the trust we place in the process of healing.

As we layer the bitter and the sweet, the layers of our lives form too. Each one, a combination of joy and sorrow, challenge and growth. Just like this dessert, it takes time for everything to come together and reach its full potential. But when we allow ourselves to embrace both sides – the sweetness and the bitterness – we create something spectacular, something worth savouring.

And so, as I share this limoncello tiramisu with you, I am reminded that no matter what we face, we can always find a way to mix the bitter with the sweet. It's in those moments of contrast that we truly find balance, and it is in the blending of both that we create the richness of our own stories. The dish, much like life, is a journey of transformation – one that, when embraced, leaves us with a sweetness that lingers long after the last bite.

This is the essence of Kneading Hope: Lessons from the Kitchen of Life – embracing the full spectrum of life's flavours, knowing that no matter how sharp the bitterness, it is always balanced by the sweetness of what comes next. Just like this tiramisu, we all have the capacity to rise, to transform, and to make something beautiful out of everything we've been through.

INGREDIENTS FOR THE FILLING:
- 2 cups mascarpone cheese
- 1/4 cup lemon curd
- 1/4 cup limoncello
- 1 lemon, zested and juiced
- 2 cups heavy whipping cream
- 1/3 cup powdered sugar

INGREDIENTS FOR THE LEMON CURD:
- 3 lemons
- 1 1/2 cups sugar
- 115g unsalted butter
- 4 extra-large eggs at room temperature
- 1/2 cup lemon juice (3 to 4 lemons)
- 1/8 teaspoon kosher salt

INGREDIENTS FOR THE SOAK:
- 3/4 cup sugar
- 4 lemons, zested and juiced
- 1/2 cup limoncello
- 2 packs of ladyfinger biscuits

INGREDIENTS FOR THE DRIZZLE:
- 1/4 cup lemon curd
- 1 tablespoon limoncello

METHOD FOR ASSEMBLING THE TIRAMISU:

• In a large bowl using a handheld mixer, cream together the mascarpone, 1/4 cup lemon curd, 1/4 cup limoncello, and the juice and zest of one lemon. Set aside.

• In another bowl using a handheld mixer, cream together the heavy whipping cream and powdered sugar until mixture thickens into peaks.

• Use a rubber spatula to gently fold the whipped cream mixture into the mascarpone mixture. Set aside.

• To make the soak, bring sugar and the juice and zest of four lemons to a boil. Reduce to a simmer and cook for 2 minutes. Turn off the heat and pour in half a cup limoncello.

• To assemble, take the ladyfingers and quickly dip them in the soak mixture, allowing them to soak up some of the liquid. Repeat with half of the ladyfingers laying them to fit in the bottom of the baking pan, cutting to fit if necessary.

• Gently scoop on half of the mascarpone mixture and spread over the ladyfingers. Repeat the layers with the remaining soaked ladyfingers, ending with the remaining half of the mascarpone filling.

• To make the drizzle, thin out 1/4 cup of lemon curd with either a tablespoon of limoncello, or remaining soak. Whisk and then carefully drizzle over top of the tiramisu.

• Cover and refrigerate for at least 4 hours or up to a day before serving.

METHOD FOR THE LEMON CURD:

• Zest three lemons, being careful to avoid the white pith.

• Add the sugar and combine until the zest is well incorporated into the sugar.

• Cream the butter and beat in the sugar and lemon mixture. Add the eggs, one at a time, and then add the lemon juice and salt. Mix until combined.

• Pour the mixture into a small saucepan and cook over low

Layers of sweetness and sourness.

heat until thickened (about 10 minutes), stirring constantly.

• The lemon curd will thicken at about 80C, or just below simmer.

• Remove from the heat and cool or refrigerate.

Blue Ribbon Travel in 1986.

The start of the Portugal stage of the Camino de Santiago.

Our travels have taken us to amazing places all over the world.

John looks like a possum caught in the headlights. In my defence, he knew the risks!

Clearly, I find it very difficult to hide the joy I feel when sharing food and stories.

Cheers to being grateful.

Wainui Falls, New Zealand.

The colours of the Italian flag are never far away.

Making pizza fritte at Designer Dirt.

Making crostelli with my niece, Evelina.

With Ann and Steven Piacun at Albany Farmers Markets.

Having a laugh with cooking class participants.

A message for all after my skydive.

Another delicious Italian-themed platter.

Speaking at a fundraiser.

What would an Italian kitchen be without a wood-fired pizza oven?

He may prefer to be in the background, but there would be no Nilla's Italian Kitchen without John.

Making lasagna with Zia Gianina.

Preparing some treats for a Breast Cancer Morning Tea.

With my "adopted grandson" Reef and Kristen. Reef is often my right-hand-man during cooking classes.

John's Perspective

A Journey of Healing, Growth and Connection for All Ages.

AS I look back on this journey with Nilla, I can't help but feel gratitude for the strength we've both found, especially in our most challenging moments.

Watching Nilla navigate the pain of loss and trying to rebuild herself from the depths of heartbreak was overwhelming and frustrating. There were times when I honestly didn't know how to help her.

Nothing was working. More than once, I thought the weight of it all was too much. I questioned whether I was strong enough to be there for her.

Gradually, over time, I noticed something incredible happening. Nilla found healing in the kitchen – not just through the meals she prepared, but through the act of sharing them. And with that, I also found a new way to connect with her. Those shared moments around the table, where food became more than sustenance, became our lifeline. Through cooking, we communicated when words fell short, found solace in each other and discovered food's healing power. Food became our anchor, our bridge and our safe space.

John hard at work in preparation for a Christmas dinner.

The real power of how food heals came from what participants shared from our cooking classes. The unexpected bonus came in the form of feedback highlighting the intense feelings of connection they felt in the sanctuary of the kitchen.

Through this pain, healing and growth, we found something beautiful – community. It isn't just about our journey; it's about creating a space where everyone, from the youngest to the oldest, can connect, share their stories and find healing through food.

Through our "Cucina Kids" program, our grandson Harvey shares his love for food with kids, helping them find joy and connection through cooking.

Then there's "Cucina Teens", where Reef shares his journey as a teenager, connecting with others his age through food and experiences.

Of course, we're bringing together people from different cultures to share their stories, recipes and traditions, building a community bound by the love of food, growth and connection.

If you've faced struggles or felt uncertain about what's next, I want you to know you're not alone. This community is about more than just recipes – it's about sharing our challenges, finding strength in each other and discovering healing through food.

If it feels right, and you are ready to explore how to start your journey with us, please be our guest. You can find an exclusive offer at www.nillasitaliankitchen.com.au/kneadinghope

Reef and Harvey are an important part of the future at at Nilla's Italian Kitchen.

You will find a community and experience how food, shared stories and connections can help you heal, grow and rebuild. It's a space where you're always welcome, no matter what you've been through.

A children's coloured pasta class at Nilla's Italian Kitchen.

In Conclusion:

A Journey from Loss to Love - The Kitchen as My Sanctuary

AS I reflect on the journey I've walked – the heartbreak, the triumphs, the loss, and the rebirth – I stand here today, filled with gratitude. Each chapter of my life, each challenge, each step has shaped me into the person I am now. From the moment I lost my Mama, to the struggles with infertility, the complexities of family and the rawness of grief, I have learned that what life takes away, it also gives back – sometimes in the most unexpected ways.

The pain of loss was never easy to endure, but it was through that very pain that I learned the most profound lessons about strength, resilience and the power of love. The business I had spent so many years building – the heart of my life – was taken away by the global pandemic, leaving me with a sense of devastation that I could hardly process. But as so often happens when the world seems to break us, new paths emerge in the ashes of what was lost.

From the depths of this loss, I found my true calling again. It was through my grief and the unravelling of everything I once knew that Nilla's Italian Kitchen was born anew. What was once a family kitchen full of love and tradition transformed into my sanctuary – a space where I could channel the heartache into something healing for others. The kitchen became more than just a place to cook; it became a place to share, to connect and to lift each other up.

Every day is an opportunity to help others find their own healing and to nourish both their bodies and spirits.

In this new chapter, every day is an opportunity to help others find their own healing and to nourish both their bodies and spirits. Nilla's Italian Kitchen is not just a place to learn recipes; it's where I pour out my heart, my lessons and my love, offering the same warmth that my family's kitchen once provided. Here, I have the privilege of creating a space for others to reconnect – not only with food but with the people they share it with. This kitchen, born from the pain of loss, has become the very place where healing begins again, one shared meal at a time.

It is through the shared love of food and the stories we create over meals that I have witnessed lives change. Every dish we create, every class we host, every laugh shared in the kitchen, has become a testament to the power of connection and the magic that food can bring to our lives. This has become my gift, my way of honouring those who came before me, and carrying forward the lessons they taught me.

The beautiful words of a dear friend echo in my heart:

> "My darling friend Nilla, I so dearly want my girls to meet you as I know that your effervescent warmth is something that will remind them of their beautiful Nonna Bianca. Their greatest loss in life was having to give up their warm and loving family in South Africa. But after every storm comes a rainbow... and we're finding our feet in this wonderful community of Albany, with rare gems like you unexpectedly coming into our lives like a precious gift from above!"

I'm constantly amazed and humbled by the fact that each class at Nilla's Italian Kitchen seems to evoke some new emotional reaction.

These words reflect exactly what Nilla's Italian Kitchen has come to represent – a place where warmth, love and food come together to form a new kind of family. The losses, the pain and the struggles I have faced have led me here, to this place where lives are touched, hearts are healed and people rediscover their joy in the simplest of things: food, community, and connection.

Through it all, I've learned that food is so much more than

If something quietly stirred or stayed with you, there's a world beyond these pages where kindred hearts gather. Visit kneadinghope.com.au/stirred when it feels right.

nourishment; it is a bridge. It's a way of bringing people together, healing old wounds and celebrating the beauty of what we have now. The kitchen, once a place of private solace for me, has become a vibrant community space where we share, laugh, and cook with love. And every moment spent teaching others, watching them discover joy in the process, feels like a precious gift – a way to share what I have learned, and what I continue to learn, with those who come through my doors.

And just as I've created this space to share my story, I invite you to join our community – where every one of you can share your own story in a safe sanctuary. Nilla's Italian Kitchen is not just a place to cook; it is a place where you can connect, heal, and grow with others who have their own stories to tell. It's where you are welcomed, embraced, and where your experiences are honoured. Together, we create something beautiful—not just in the kitchen, but in our lives.

So, where am I now? I am in a place of peace, purpose, and gratitude.

This is a legacy of the love, strength and resilience that was passed down to me through the generations. It is a legacy I will continue to share – one meal, one lesson, one heart at a time.

You are always welcome here at Nilla's Italian Kitchen, where food, family and connection are the heart of everything we do.

Acknowledgements

SITTING here reflecting on the words that have filled these pages, my heart is overflowing with love and gratitude. This journey has been shaped by the unwavering support of so many incredible people: John, Jason, Lisa and Harvey, whose love and strength have lifted me through every moment. I'm deeply thankful to my family, friends, past staff and clients, who have been part of this beautiful journey, helping me build something meaningful over the years. I also feel immense gratitude for my students, whose presence in my cooking classes continues to bring joy and connection.

The Camino taught me resilience, and the medical system that saved my life and helped me walk again has been a lifeline. I am also forever grateful for the memories left by my Mama, Papa and brother – those memories have been the foundation of my strength and purpose.

Every memory, every challenge and every lesson along the way has brought me to this moment where I can share a message of hope with you. If it weren't for all these experiences, the love and the connections, I wouldn't be able to sit here now and say that, in the end, everything truly works out for the best.

Let the sun shine on you and, if you can see the heart in the rays, know that it is my heart that is with you!

Grazie di cuore!

(Thank you from the bottom of my heart)

Nilla x